Conscience – The Super Ego

Foreword

The mouse was getting to be too much.

The cartoonists working for Walt Disney were tired of coming up with stories for Mickey Mouse and couldn't dissuade Disney to get rid of the mouse so one of them remembered an old Italian novel, really a moral fable, about a puppet-maker by the name of Geppetto who made a wooden puppet and named him Pinocchio.

After completing Pinocchio and putting him on a shelf in his workshop, Geppetto went to bed and slept. That night, a fairy by the name of the Blue Fairy rid the puppet of his strings and enlivened him, promising that if he proved himself worthy, he would become a real boy. To help him in his quest, she appointed an insect by the name of Jiminy Cricket to be his conscience.

Jiminy's job was to notify Pinocchio whenever he was about to get into trouble. The film had some catchy tunes and some noble phrases such as "Let your conscience be your guide."

In spite of meeting up with some unsavory characters, Pinocchio in the end did become a real boy, thanks to Jiminy Cricket.

Many generations of young boys and girls have grown up affected by that movie. In a very simplistic way, it tells how

1

conscience is developed by doing good deeds.

There are many people today who believe that we are born with a conscience – that we know right from wrong within us from our very first breath. It's an easy way to condemn anyone to prison. A way to be sure computers never are wrong. Human beings never make mistakes is their belief.

For those who accept that all human beings do make mistakes and we have to take that into account when passing judgment, let's join with them in hoping and praying for a God who practices that in passing final judgment on all of us.

Chapter 1

That thing that comes out a woman's womb is a creature, living, breathing and announcing his/her existence in this world. He/she is a human being, with a body and a soul. The body is seen, the soul is unseen but known because it is a life force, a principle of existence.

That human being must be raised, provided nourishment and care to survive. He/she develops, that body growing older as time goes on. Muscle, bone, skin and organs expanding as existence continues on, the cells carrying out their functions. The human being can be called that thing, the Id, the basic existence.

As that human being is existing and acting out its existence, it becomes a person, an Ego, a personality to distinguish its behavior.

When the brain cells in the head get to making connections between using the information collected with doing the actions he/she wants to do, then we have a Super Ego, a decision-maker, a person responsible for his/her actions. That life force, the soul, has an attribute the Creator of matter and spirit imbued in it to be exercised when reasoning is functioning.

All the influences that affect the thinking or reasoning can act on the emotions or feeling. We don't know why one part of the brain can get a bigger charge than another but memory circuits can store minute bits of information that can be dredged up because of a certain trigger by a part of the brain which is reacting. The number of brain cells prevent artificial manipulation from continually controlling any part of the brain.

What is of concern are all the outside influences that can affect one's thinking and feeling. Is it awareness or curiosity that draws two creatures to make another creature? Does curiosity arouse the need to survive, to create another creature? Or are the creatures aware of differences in their bodies and shapes and want to take advantage of the differences to make another creature? There are egos involved because of the differences. What the two creatures seek is something of each of them showing and acting in the new creature. Even if the two creatures do not share in producing another creature, they may still look for shares of themselves in the new creature. A person may want a pet animal that acts the way they want. These wants, desires and acts we call being =arent or guardian and hopefully the parents will care for the creature to nourish and educate until the creature can take care of itself.

As the creature grows, curiosity interests him/her into learning about other creatures. Using more and more brain cells, the creature distinguishes between known and unknown creatures.

4

The known nourish and train him/her in behavior and personal hygiene. Behavior is control and punishment is avoidance. The multitude of creatures the creature himself/herself encounters are grouped in his/her learning to be known as family, comprising those seen and lived with everyday and those seen only on visits.

Besides general groupings, the creature learns about relationships, experiencing age differences and living differences. Being in the same house or shelter means learning about how to act with other creatures and knowing about oneself whereby one becomes a person or individual with a way of acting or having a personality. We see stages of development. At age two, a person can rebel against the learning of and adjusting to expected behavior. Training may be needed at every waking hour, not only for behavior but personal hygiene as well. Hopefully, by age three the person will learn to control oneself, both in body and mind, otherwise the training must continue until control is realized.

Chapter 2

The reason for speaking of an infant as a creature until childhood is reached is to make the ascent into personhood a major change. Training an infant is far different than training a child because rejection to change takes place in childhood. Freedom of will needs guidance for acceptance of responsibility.

Learning to talk is a good thing. Learning to lie is a bad thing. The guardians and relatives of the child provide guidance to the child. Any faults in guiding a child are the responsibility of the guardians and relatives.

A child usually advances to the student stage. The child is learning but the teaching can be done by other persons than his/her parents, relatives and friends.

By attending a school, a child comes into contact with teachers and schoolmates. He/she is exposed to formal learning, set subjects that teach how to read, write and count, the basics.

As adults, too often we forget children learn individually and we try to put them through a factory of learning. All children are to come out the same, learning all the same in the same way and thinking and acting in the same way.

One popular movement today thinks a machine, a computer, can teach each child in his/her own way. If we can produce cars, televisions and phones and individualize production, then we can individualize the production of taught children, some people think and believe.

The outcome is the reasoning that if a child doesn't learn how to read, count and write, it's the fault of the individual because he/she doesn't want to learn.

Carrying that thinking over to the formation of conscience, we come up with the thinking that the child wants to misbehave, the child wants to reject control. The child is bound to get into not only present but future trouble. He/she is just no good.

Without guidance, the child can grow up to misbehave, to mistrust others, to take advantage of others, to harm others. We can't expect an infant or a child to realize that he/she didn't get here on their own or that they need help to develop and grow in both body, mind and soul. As they live and act and learn, they have to be taught and guided.

While the child is being taught and guided, he/she can be influenced by hundreds, maybe even thousands of people. He/she will have schoolmates, friends, doctors, nurses, religious people, neighbors, random acquaintances and strangers to have him/her realize the vast numbers of different persons by age, sex, race, color, creed, nationality and whatever else can make them different.

But, as Pinocchio learned in his adventures, there are good

people and there are bad people. The factory-minded people think either God made people that way or that people made themselves that way. The blame is on all the influences that helped grow the person that way.

We can argue round and round about why there are good people and bad people but there is one finality: death. Because of death there is time. Time has history, both people and events. All things and people have an end. We can talk of birth but we know there is an end- death.

Death can remind us of conscience. If there is an end, then there should be a judgment. Because we can reason, we can think things out. We have done some things well and some things not so well. If there is judgment, then there is a judge.

Since we can think, we can deny anything, except death. We don't have to accept death. Death will happen no matter what. In the meantime, we can think and believe what we want and do or not do what we want or not want

We can deny history. We can deny creation. We can deny a Creator. Why can we accept or deny? Because we are free to do so. It's strange that the people who most deny free will are the ones that most want laws. Laws never tell us what to do. They command us what not to do. Laws limit what we can do or deny us from doing things.

We live in a time when there is more knowledge, more communication, more ways to travel, more ways to learn, better health, more conveniences to make life and work easier, more education available, yet many people find it fashionable to deny everything and anything, even that they have a conscience.

I can deny there is a creator. Everything has been around for centuries. All of it just came to be on its own, I can believe. All those planets and stars just hang there, like they've been hanging there for centuries. How can I be sure we've landed a mobile machine on Mars? It could be on some desert in Mongolia, for all we know. After all, we have designed and made machines that can move mountains Why should we worry how long the sun can last? It's been burning a long time and still is big as ever way up in the sky. It's only been six hundred years since somebody said that earth is spinning around the sun instead of it spinning around us.

Is is fashion that prompts us to deny? Or is it a lack of knowledge? There is a movement to eliminate links on the servers of computers: these bits of information have nothing to do with these other bits. Everything happening today is random. There are no connections between people, places and things, the unconnected would plead. People wanting links on the servers contend that there are connections and say it is irrational not to have them . Life does have order. We live with events happening every day. Those events have a purpose. There are memories of how our lives are lived. They are our own histories.

Today we have photographs to remind us of growth and development, events that took place, things as they were in the past. We have videotapes, video discs, USBs, films, as well as photo albums to remind us, to keep our memories if our brains forget.

What the computer proves, it can also disprove. The computer can change pictures. It can remodel not only pictures of houses, it can remodel people. We have computers that can make human parts that work in a human body. We can put knowledge in a computer that will beat a human brain in a contest of knowing things. We have computers that help us send things way up in space and bring them back safely to earth. You might say a computer can delay death by analyzing a health problem and coming up with proper treatment to cure an ailment. But the computer can't stop death.

We can wash the hard drive on a computer and clean out the data stored, if we want to. There is a disease called Alzheimer's that can wipe out the brain cells that store memories and eventually destroy the controls over the body's organs. We seek a cure for the disease in order to maintain good health. For conscience, the cure is admission of guilt and change of behavior to do good and avoid evil. History tells us this is so just as it relates the cases in which evil continued.

Chapter Three

Religion is not only an admission of a life force giving us life but is also a realization that we are not alone. There are other human beings and things that are here living with us. For as many dark philosophers that have preached the worthlessness of existence, there have been many more that admit to the value of having the fullness of creation and existence.

Education should be of two types. One to teach us of creation. The other of why there is creation.

If we do not come to know of these things or do not take them seriously, we shall experience history repeating itself, if we study past events.

In the previous chapter when discussing using a computer to individualize instruction, the declaration was the computer cannot match personal instruction. The reason is that the acquisition of knowledge can be affected by the interpretation of that knowledge passed on by another human being.

Just as news events can be slanted by the arrangement of words in a sentence or sentences in a paragraph, so the presentation of learning can have bias or confusion instead of clear and honest comprehension. The younger the child, the more openness to take in whatever is presented.

Any country that denies or falsifies education to its persons from infancy through childhood and through adulthood is making itself ripe for revolution in the future. Education is learning about order. If there is no order, then creation falls in on itself and disorder rules. If the laws do not serve persons, then the laws must be changed because disorder leads to dissension and then to revolution.

For conscience, disorder is confusion. Nothing seems right because things aren't operating the same as before or the way they should. Change is good but confusion obscures the natural order. Dissension brings on more confusion. Is the way back to order the same as before? No, the path has changed. Order remains the same but the learning is different because of the circumstances that have arisen.

Free will has allowed for changes because circumstances change actions and outcomes. What is called conservative means no change is allowed. What is called liberal means too much change to fit the circumstances. This is why education must be broad, to take in changes and circumstances because of free will.

Education cannot be just for the job or just for a change. Creation is more than one person or one thing. We're just starting to learn more about our universe. What would we do with persons from other planets or other universes? Do we refuse to learn or do we look forward to learning about other creation?

Even with the universe we have, are we interested in the why of creation? Why are all these people and things here? The ancient Egyptians and Greeks proclaimed an afterlife. The good must be rewarded and the bad punished even after death here. Though pagans concentrated on their present for enjoyments only, many had good gods and bad gods, intimating that somebody (gods) will be around after death to dispense good things and bad things, the majority opting for mostly good things because the calamities that befell them in this life were catastrophic in their estimation.

The vast amount of creation made ancient peoples realize that no human person had enough power to create. This fact is evident by how women have been treated through the ages. Birth came through the woman but how much reverence was shown to her except to marvel at birth itself.

Very few times was a god made to be a female one. Males are stronger and smarter, it was thought by all the males. Men are just a step below the gods whereas the females are conniving and tempting men to defy the gods, to place themselves as equals, according to the literature and stories of the times, as if females have a different conscience than men and lead men astray. So the why of creation is confusing because females are in contention with males. Not only do females bear children, they also educate them. How many times in literature and history are women blamed for wars and pestilence instead of men who are not blamed for exercising their strength or not using their brains?

The study of ancient and modern cultures reflect this still prevalent thinking: males know what to do but females lead them astray. The truth is the bodies may be different but the souls aren't. Yet the women who are the birthers are considered criminals for even thinking about abortion.

If there is sexual abuse or rape, the female is blamed because she evidently allowed or enticed the male into the act. In law, whether moral or legislated, the woman is held to be a moral agent with legal rights but not having a moral right to abortion. She is forced to want the fetus because there is no removal of something not wanted. If the fetus dies because of some natural deficiency, the woman may be excused but the question remains: had she taken every precaution to preserve the fetus until some kind of birth could take place?

The arguments are for the sake of argument. Males are briefly educated, if at all, about respecting females because of their ability to develop creatures which can become persons. Females are briefly, if at all, educated about the care and raising

15

of persons (which should be done for males as well). We don't need separate instruction for this. Education today has forgotten the basis of society: persons come together to be families to nourish, care and educate the young until adulthood. Each person is responsible to maintain this standard. Otherwise, society breaks down and social problems become widespread.

Besides taking care of the young, another reason for families is to respect and preserve relationships between persons. Whether males with males, females with females, transgenders with their choice of sex, as well as males with females, there is a craving to love as well as being loved. Responsible sexuality must be observed and practiced in order for respect to be followed and given.

Sexual activity is very simple. The relationships that may result from the activity can be very complex and confusing. Cherished literature throughout the ages, such as the Bible, reveal many of the complexities. Ancient cultures recorded by historians of the times reveal even more complexities. Climate has some effect on nudity but this seems to be more a matter of custom. The complexities arise because of two canals: the sperm canal and the birth canal. Over centuries, these two canals have interacted to help produce creatures. Some cultures have mutilated them externally to try and control the owners of them from having sexual activity. In the early teens, young persons are aroused to find out about these two canals. The young are cautioned by older persons to control arousals because troubles can and will happen.

We are seeing in nursing homes today that older persons with dementia are being aroused and having sexual activity. This is becoming a problem because relatives of these older persons are objecting to nursing home staffs allowing the sexual activity to take place, whether married or not and even in homosexual and lesbian situations. The professional consultants, such as psychologists, serving these nursing homes, see no problem in allowing sexual activity as long as there is no abuse or coercion involved.

It seems that losing judgment and decision-making doesn't interfere with sexual arousal. This was true when we locked up in mental institutions the almost non-existent I.Q. Individuals and had to keep +he sexes locked apart from each other.

What does all this mean for conscience? Without rational decision-making and judgment, how can conscience operate? Without a functioning mind, there is a creature who is a threat to himself/herself as well as to others and whom we've named a monster if he/she exhibits aggressive behavior.

In order to have rational decision-making and judgment,

17

there must be education and teaching not only of the basics of learning but also about respect. War destroys respect as well as endangering learning. War is about pain and death. Respect must be learned not only by teaching but by example and practice as well. Respect is honoring a person for being a member of society. Respect is confirming that there is truth and honesty in our dealings with one another.

The best place for learning and practicing respect is in one's own family. Whether a group of persons is together because of relationships or whether instead of relationships by a cause or course of action, care should be taken to avoid a philosophy that propagandized in the latter part of the twentieth century that called for exploiting oneself in order to strengthen one's own personality. Instead of developing and encouraging mutual support and respect, emphasis was placed on giving free play to one's own feelings and emotions to the neglect of respect for other persons. If we are feeling low or depressed, we were told it was our own fault. Money was to be made in large sums if we just looked in the mirror and told ourselves of how great we are. Our cleverness provided us with the honesty and respect due us for being better than anyone else. We would succeed in spite of the family that raised us if we practiced taking advantage of others in order to overcome any feelings of guilt or concern for others.

We need divorce so the state decides who should take care of the children and what they should be taught. The companies that employ us should have control of our personal lives, denying women contraceptive medication so they are responsible for immorality during work or after. Government should stay out of our lives (why is it passing all these laws that seem to be taking control of us?) This is where our own cleverness has led us.

We are social persons. We each have a conscience. When we go looking for a mate, we hope for the best combination of sex and love to satisfy our cravings for perfection.

Back when the immigrant population overwhelmed the established groupings, the maxims circulated in the neighborhoods were concerned with dating and marrying our own kind. The favorite saying was to date the girl or boy next door. To stray from the neighborhood, even across town, was to invite danger. Culture and religion held sway for anywhere from an eighth to a quarter of the town.

When metropolises sprang up as a result of overcrowded and sprawling neighborhoods, culture and religion squeezed into the compact housing areas to remain the dominant determiners of securing mates.

When a great war came and took millions of young first, second and third generation of men and removed them for years from their old neighborhoods, changes began in those generations even though the neighborhoods remained the same except for enough mates not being available and time demanding a long patience to wait for their return.

As was previously said, war destroys respect and brings pain and death. It wasn't just the males who experienced pain and death. The families did too in many different ways. Culture and religion, through propaganda, were modified to fit the great war and events.

At the conclusion of the war, disorder ceased to be a great problem but confusion remained because decisions needed to be made. Surprisingly, the biggest decision was how soon should everything return to normal.

The past was gone and because it was so upsetting would try to be forgotten. Changes were taking place in rapid sequence as new neighborhoods were set up at a distance from the old ones. Education was going to be available to an expanding population and advances to comfortable living were happening as housing and transportation satisfied new needs. The girl next door got married but she no longer lived there. She became the suburban mother of three to five children and the father of the children drove his car to work for almost an hour's travel time from the family dwelling. The telephone and the automobile made the family more mobile. The nineteen-fifties remained fairly stable for family living.

The Vietnam War was a war nobody wanted. It changed many lives over more than forty years. The killing and being killed in the war became part of living. Truth and morality were not topics for conversation because events seemed unreal. The end of the war was so confusing that nobody could believe it was over. Death had been so prevalent that religion lost its appeal and an emptiness filled in. The leaders in government pretended to be in charge of events and to encourage people to partake of modern living with its luxuries but the emptiness remained.

The creep of the philosophy of exploitation steadily messaged our brains with the promise of individual strength overcoming the burden of social justice. Let things happen and everything will straighten out alright.

A brief interlude interrupted the full force of exploitation and a balanced prosperity seemed to be happening as business corporations found themselves having to defend against rapacious paper-shufflers who threatened takeovers based on junk values. Employees feared for their jobs if a takeover happened but in many companies the employees had a stake in the company and their worth was of more value than the junk values being offered so the employees' value won out and eventually the junk market evaporated.

All went well until there was an election one night when the voters went to bed thinking an outcome would be ready by the morning of their awakening but in the morning there was no conclusion, no outcome. Many days later a decision was made that to many was contrary to past history and unreality set in.

War happened and confusion returned. The war was unreal except to those who fought in it. Reality ceased in daily life as lying became the protective cloak of the government of the people. Yet patriotism was drummed into the ears of the people to make the scenes play out in daily life as if all was well in governance. Upholding all the laws was stressed even as the prisons were stuffed with the convicted who were never to be reformed as a supposed cost-saving measure. Is it any wonder that confusion reigned? War is not for the weak. The only strength is boxcars of bombs and bullets. Respect becomes being on the winning side because might makes right, proven over tens of years of wars.

Chapter Four

How does a family hold up against such onslaughts as war and disrespect? Is it any wonder that the family draws in upon itself to find the strength to persevere?

We are told that in spite of a birthrate of less than two the population is expanding. As we wonder how this can be, we forget the waves of immigration from lands where the leaders have no connection and no respect for their own dwellers so that those people flee to lands where some sort of peace is part of daily living.

Arriving at a place where there is peace, refugees sense an obligation to enlarge their families by increasing births and sending for more relatives. Veterans returning from wars seem to have that same sense of survival and the desire to start families or increase births.

After two or three years in a peaceful environment and through the influence of local living conditions and television, circumstances may change the thinking and attitudes of the newcomers to the extent that women seek out employment to be wage-earners and consider health issues as to the number of children they should have. With the labor-saving devices for maintaining a household and feeding a family, many women experience changes in their responsibilities in caring for their families. Religion may challenge their new realizations of their changing roles and attitudes while their off-springs are freely fitting into new lifestyles and friendships. The males generally do not want to allow changes in attitudes and traditions for the entire family and may use religion as the measure to fight any changes.

Since in most religions males are the leaders and guides in policy formation and traditions to follow is it any wonder that family members are questioning whether the old ways are to be kept or if the new realities are demanding changes?

Veterans returning from wars have experienced things beyond the normal way of life and want to settle down and return to some normalcy reminiscent of their former life. Their difficulty is in trying to explain to their families what abnormalities they experienced in performing their duties.

For both refugees and returning warriors, the past had an influence on their lives and their thinking. Though they try to put the past aside, their new environment and circumstances never alter past memories.

In psychology, the only reason for going back to the past is to admit to what happened and to go on, hopefully for the better. Going back is to admit to making a mistake or to try and answer why something happened. In life, the axiom to best live by is not to make the same mistake twice.

When it comes to religion, going back in time is an admission of imperfection. Somewhere back then a sin was committed. Whether major or minor, an imperfection occurred and guilt came shuddering down.

For example, a teenager discovers seminal fluid discharges when he is sleeping. This is a new occurrence in his advance towards adulthood. He questions an older teenager and is told not to worry about it since it's part of growing up.

Upset over the fact that he had no control of his body yet the discharge happened, he questions an old adult who tells him it's probably his fault for reading girlie magazines or watching an adult program on television where naked female bodies are shown and his imagination places what he's seen in his mind which conjures up a scene involving him and making him react sexually

Now feeling guilt over possibly having instigated the problem during his awareness activities, he discusses the happening with a clergyman who counsels him to pray for forgiveness for his offense and to avoid occasions in which he might be tempted to take pleasure in observing indecent exposures.

Believing that his introduction to sex in this way is a failing in his personal morality, the teenager without further counseling can develop an attitude that anything to do with sex is sinful, or an attitude that sex is part of living that is to be taken advantage of in order to learn about the opposite sex since he doesn't give birth to babies and males have little to do with raising them.

He may consider himself moral without realizing he isn't respecting himself or others if he hasn't been guided properly. Passing a law to teach morality is as useless as making a list of actions that are sinful. When conscience is made a Super-man instead of a Super-ego, then we believe that we look out for ourselves and forget about everybody else.

Many people wouldn't believe that the Bible is a psychology book. Most think of it as a storybook or as something sacred like the Ten Commandments in stone. But if you want to find out about many of the depravities of people, the Bible is a history of lies, deceits, killings, wars, and general mistreatment of other people as well as having lessons in forgiveness, respect for others and love of others.

Even modern novel writers can be intrigued when the Bible relates the tale of the ruler who kills his best friend after promising a young woman anything she wants because of her tantalizing dance before the ruler and at the suggestion of her mother who hates the best friend since he knows of her infidelities and sinful ways.

Or the general who desires the wife of one of his subordinates and sees to it that the man is put into the front line where he most likely will be killed and the general woos his wife while she mourns her husband's death.

Can we be so taken by the stories that we ignore thinking of what those instigators did and how they convinced their consciences of the good of their actions? In modern times, we still aren't sure how a mass murderer can walk into a building and kill people and say he didn't realize what he was doing because he was playing out a part in his imagination. We may kill the murderer but that doesn't deter others from doing it. We are so modern that we can't realize why humans have free will.

Chapter Five

Alas! The poor teenager! Not yet an adult but confronted with complex situations! At school, new friends and/or new relationships call for decision-making. Who do I want to be friends with and will they want me as a friend? If becoming friends means a different kind of love than what I have experienced in my family, how do I react with that friend of a different sex or the same sex but not like between me and my brother or sister or mother or father? How can I just like someone and our relationship is not the same as being brother or sister because we don't live together and aren't related by blood or birth?

Yet if I want a closer relationship than friendship, how do I behave with my partner? I want a closeness that might involve sex.

The parents of these teenagers are in a group called "boomers", people born from 1960 to 1980 and a little beyond. In various magazine articles, the "boomers" are described as parents whose parents advised them when teenagers to "keep your pants zipped up" or "keep your legs crossed" and not much else, hoping the birth control pill made sex less daring.

Now the "boomer" parents figured the pill would relieve the tensions of the teen years and education and television would bring on maturity to their pampered and indulged youths.

After all, the "boomer" parents weren't the wild drug experimenters and anti-war protesters of the 1960's, the frustrated and distressed witnesses of the famous murders and disgraced and comical politicians of the 1970's. They endured the apathy and the money crazes of the 1980's with a quiet determination to endure the break-ups in many families and profess true love and enduring partnership with their chosen spouse as they set about to start a family.

Many males and females couldn't find a desired or compatible mate and would remain single, though they may have connected with someone and had a creature or two together that usually the female raised on her own.

These young adults had usually been pampered by their parents, especially with the break-up of many families, so they pampered their offspring and made a point of celebrating holidays together to continue traditions.

Both the couples and the singles saw the changes in employment practices and the lack of trust of employees in a company so they decided that the number of children to best care for should be limited to one or two and rarely three or four. The politicians fought for expanding the economy and families and denied the right of a female to choose whether to become pregnant or to continue to develop a creature, regardless of her personal health or her will to choose. The politicians did more than deny. They kept attempting to force a woman to have children by attacking abortion. Many religions chimed in, trying to intimidate females by telling them how guilty they should be for even thinking about contraception and abortion.

Males were predominant in both politics and religion. Again, the thinking was that females are not smart enough to think for themselves so males have to pass laws or preach against freedom of choice. Even with doctors in politics, they followed the political line and passed laws narrowing contraception and almost eliminating legal abortion while they enjoyed their golf games by increasing the number of cesarean births rather than natural childbirth.

Many couples and singles found job occupations with reduced pay, a practice that had been taking place for over twenty years since the 1960's. With housing prices rising because of less new construction and fewer homes available, the cost of raising a family continued to rise even if wages didn't. Even in two wage-earner families where the costs of feeding, clothing and providing shelter were barely adequate to provide a family with time together and the costs of new electronic gadgets, there was little time to be a family by sharing culture, religion, education and morality.

What really caused the collapse of American culture was the unjust decision of the Supreme Court to end the 2000 election. What took place that November night in Tennessee will be known only by future generations but the harm persists. The supposition for what took place in the dark early morning hours after the election had to do with the vote count in Florida where the ballot had several flaws. During the recount, requested because of the flaws, the Supreme Court stepped in and declared the winner, a shock to the electorate which had always been told that every single vote counts.

Since then, the Supreme Court has allowed employers, on religious grounds, to interfere with their female employees' right to practice birth control (which implies the Supreme Court sets moral standards by allowing employers to control freedom of choice). It hearkens back to school boards in the 1930's firing female teachers for wearing slacks instead of dresses.

Now we can say that what occurred in the 1930's had no effect on the miniskirts of the 1970's because there were three wars in between two generations but did the overlaps with the

31

generations provide fresh air for new thinking on culture and morality? After all, the children of the 1930's were raised in an atmosphere of strict obedience but in the 1950's there was a slight loosening of morality that burst open in the 1960's.

What brings on these comparisons is remembering what the sayers said of conscience: it's born in us and has the basics from the very beginning of conception, declared as gospel. We can deny that events had nothing to do with changes in thinking (because we have free will) but curiosity weighs on the mind as to the effect of major events on culture, religion and morality.

Today the assault on veracity and reality has resulted in an attack on trust. Trust no one because trust requires respect and vice versa. No respect: no trust. No trust: no respect. No respect: nothing is real; anything can be denied; relationships are lies, fakes to be exploited by the strong and distrusting.

How is trust restored? When love is gone, there is no feeling. The emotions in the brain are jangling. They need to know someone loves you. There is another person that cares about you. There is somebody willing to care for you. Things will get better if there are two persons instead of one. That is the secret of being persons instead of creatures.

How can a female give birth to a creature and not want it? Because there is no other person to share it with, to love it and to care for it.

You can't accept God unless you accept another person. Relationship is based on accepting other persons.

When a baby dies because of a body malfunction, there is grief because it was a person becoming. The soul, the life-force, has gone away. When a child dies because of an illness or accident, the grief seems even greater because the person becoming was closer to being a person but the soul, the life-force, has gone away.

No matter how many movies are made, pretending the soul comes back in another body, death will again occur sometime. So the question is why come back again since the overwhelming belief for centuries has been that there is a forever after this existence?

Of course, because of free will, there are many who deny there is a forever. But if there is no forever, there is nothing and who wants to be nothing? Strangely, the deniers boast about the weirdest of ideas like predestination, but who wants a destiny of eventually being nothing?

Chapter Six

In terrible economic times, it is difficult to move around. Wages are barely enough to cover the cost of living and savings are almost impossible. Housing is tight because there is little money to afford a house or a car. Not moving around much allows school age children to have schoolmates and possibly make friends. Apartment living, caused by low wages, can result in moving within a city or county to find affordable shelter and making it difficult for children to develop friendships, or the family to have the time to care and share for each other. Military families especially have problems not only in finding housing but in maintaining a stable environment for children to attend school and make friends when base assignments may change every nine months. Cell phones and the internet have helped somewhat to maintain friendships if they have previously been established.

Mobility may not be as extensive as in the past when it comes to distances involved but circumstances are changing the togetherness within families because of the movement of family members. There is less time for parents to be with their children either because of work, social doings or just not enough time to be together within a dwelling.

Things are changing and people don't know where to look for advice. Many adults can't find friends or the time to discuss problems or situations to figure a course of action or solution. At work, there are fewer people working together or are taken up by tasks and there's no time for discussion. Within a family dwelling, there seems to be less attention to each other and less interest in what is happening to each.

Messages can go back and forth on cell phones and the internet but there is less trust between individuals and less care and sharing. There is less acceptance of any solutions to a problem or situation.

Everything seems compartmentalized. Is there a pill or a book of advice that will take care of the problem or at least alleviate some of the distress or possibly eliminate it?

The how-to books have changed from making money to getting people to like one another and getting them to work as a team. The pills no longer energize us. They look after our specific health needs.

We communicate with our friends and acquaintances by electronic means more than by face-to-face. We are ashamed to discuss personal problems because we think of them as failures of our personality.

We believe in divorce as a means to end disagreements in our relationships and to allow us to seek out new partners in our quest for the perfect match.

Are we changing or is the world changing and we are just going along with it? As we listen to the news each week, we hear of the lack of trust. People are killing other people. People are defaming other persons of note. Countries don't want to help other countries . We may want to put in a security system in our houses to protect us under our roofs and all our goods. Do we even trust ourselves? Can we deceive even ourselves?

Pride is like a snake that comes out and bites us when we least expect it.

Pride is like Pharaoh's charioteers seeing the tribes of Israel on the other bank and the walls of the Red Sea towering over them and thinking: "Wait until we get there and we'll show them a thing or two. We'll beat them up real good."

Pride is seeing a penniless person on the street and thinking: "I'm so much better than him!"

Pride is not the same as when we are depressed and need to see the blue sky and a bright sun up above.

Pride is not caring about other people. Charles Dickens told us that Ebeneezer Scrooge changed when he saw Marley's ghost. It was a stepping-stone to seeing the benefit of caring for other people. After all, who believes in ghosts? Or was it Scrooge's conscience that made him remember the good times with Jacob Marley and how they ran an honest and caring business? The main point is living a caring and sharing life now instead of just in the past.

While growing in the teen years, what needs to be learned are our moral obligations to each other so that as adults we live and practice caring and sharing and respecting each other.

On television, when we see Europeans nuzzling each other on both cheeks, that doesn't preclude them from having at each other with rapiers when tempers flare. Or, with Orientals, from bowing reverently before each other and then slamming each other with kicks when there is a dispute.

Here in America, we may shake hands but we can slug each other in a fight when we don't see eye-to-eye on certain issues.

All of these are not ideals to learn but, being physical, we know that proper behavior should be taught not just at home but followed in public as well. So morality must be taught because our moral obligations are to more than our family members and our schoolmates.

We think we are so modern that good old-fashioned ways are outmoded in today's society.

As teenagers in school, do we just have schoolmates or do we have friends too? Stealing from another student's locker doesn't build trust or true sharing. Spreading ugly rumors or bullying another student isn't caring about others. And enticing another student into having sex isn't showing respect. These obligations to trust, share, care and respect others must be practiced in daily living because becoming adults doesn't change basic behavior. Conscience is still being formed even in the teen years.

What is the reward of forming a right conscience? It's very simple. It's goodness.

Evil is not to be joked about. It gets us into much trouble. To be a good person is to be admired for being a true person, a true friend, a true lover.

To continue that goodness through life makes life worth living.

Just because we finish basic education at the end of high school doesn't mean we are adults.

Chapter Seven

Does conscience age as we grow older? It's not really aging. It's experiencing more things or doing something more times as we live life.

For those who would expect a book on sex or love-making, this isn't. There are multitudes of fictional and non-fictional stories of such in literature, especially in these times.

More importantly, does conscience belong to the body or to the soul, the life-force? In this day and age, the problem is trying to determine death. For now, we will support the theory that death occurs when brain activity ceases.

The definition of becoming an adult is when development of the body and its organs are completed. We are then considered ripe or mature. Aging stops developing and from then on there is decline.

Science today is sophisticated enough to take cells from the body and grow some new parts and replace parts but eventually the parts decline. Science is experimenting with DNA chains to remove bad molecules that make illnesses and move good or better DNA to make a better creature. But death is still final.

So the body develops to a certain point and then it stops. What about the mind? Every day brain cells die and new ones are activated. Does that indicate the mind is taking over the body? No, because when it comes to unfamiliar risks (a broad category that encompasses making new acquaintances, sex, body health and accidents), there can be disjointed action between rational habits and virtuous habits.

Habits start way back when we are infants. One of the strongest habits is distinguishing between right and wrong and in infancy it's a matter of reward and punishment: do what I tell you or show you and you won't be punished.

Virtue is too often described as a commitment to act but a better definition is a capacity to act which allows for a hesitation of the mind to decide before making a final judgment.

When we get to an age where we start to meet more persons and our curiosity is aroused as to whether a person should be merely an acquaintance or a friend or more than a friend, our infantile neuroses must be overcome by finding out whether this person we're interested in is good for us to know and form a relationship with or not worth knowing more about and not forming any kind of relationship.

In conversing with a person, we may find the data our mind is taking in is making us form feelings for that person and, hopefully, there are mutual feelings in turn to interest both of us into some kind of relationship. Our thinking mind is distinguishing between likes and dislikes, things we have in common or not at all, and storing the comparisons for future reference so we can have rational habits to fall back on, depending on our reaction to the data and the actions we take as a result.

Storing experiences affects our imaginations to expand our knowledge and behavior in future relations with another person or many others. The experiences may take in thoughts, actions, desires and feelings in dealing with others.

Sex may lead our feelings, curiosity and imagination to wonder what a real relationship with another person would be like, especially when one person has a semen canal and the other a birth canal in their physical selves. Depending on all the factors involved in their developments, two persons are confronted with making a decision as to whether joining bodies is a reward for following rational habits or a feeling of guilt for not following virtuous habits of honest good towards one another. For those of the same sex, the question of a physical relationship exists as well and a mutual decision still needs to be made.

The final determinant in making a decision should be dependent on a spiritual equilibrium. When the rational habits are indeterminate with the virtuous habits, the life-force, the soul, should be considered in making the decision. There can be no equilibrium without the involvement of the life-force, the soul. There is no way of eliminating guilt except by admitting that the life-force was ignored and will be considered in future resolutions and decisions.

Not just sexual actions and relationships are concerned with spiritual equilibrium. Job responsibilities, family relationships, neighborhood concerns, city, state and federal issues, any dealings with other persons where honest good is under consideration should acknowledge that our life-forces, our souls, are involved as well as our physical selves.

Generally we look to people we know for advice on what we are to do or have done. But if there is guilt where forgiveness is necessary, then the counsel of persons who are familiar with the workings of the life-force, the soul, may be best sought.

In the example of the teenager who talked to the old adult and was told to "forget it", the teen sought the advice of a clergyman and was told to pray for forgiveness. The clergyman's response is like a doctor telling a patient: "you have a problem but take care of it yourself". The clergyman declines to be involved. The clergyman should be a doctor of the life-force, the soul, and should handle the teen's problem by counseling and maybe making a referral to another counselor if necessary. Seeking the advice of a friend is asking for concern and involvement in a personal matter. But this is why there are other persons on this planet with us.

In becoming adults and experiencing life's changes, the solution to remaining normal is by fitting in and adjusting to all the persons we encounter. No two persons are exactly alike. Free will enlivens daily living with daily proof that habits have to be developed over time to take into account any changes in routine. In this existence, there is good and there is evil. Evil is the abuse of honest good. Good is doing what we are supposed to do in helping others as well as ourselves.

When we become adults, we are no longer growing up but acting out what we've learned. In law, this is recognized by emancipating a person who, even underage, has demonstrated the ability to adapt to life's circumstances. The person is ready to care and support himself/herself without dependence on another person. Medically, we could consider the birth of a baby as emancipation from the womb of a woman after the cutting of the umbilical cord. In religion, the question of when the soul enters the body has been argued for centuries but the description of the soul as a life-force indicates infusion at birth rather than life only beginning at cell fusion since conditions up to and including birth can affect development.

Somewhere between the ages of ten and twelve, we realized we weren't children anymore, like back in the primary grades where we had to follow the teacher's direction otherwise we would be clumsy and lost. We had to expand our vocabulary and learn to think a little more to handle the difference between words and numbers.

As teens, we learned to be careful so we didn't look foolish to our classmates. We found sharing ideas and feelings were expanding our little world and we had to learn how to get along or stay off to the side. High school meant body and mind working with thoughts, words and actions to survive where atonement and forgiveness were either learned or hurt and guilt were deeply experienced as a portent of what the adult world was like. We learned what adaptation means, either adjusting to others or to situations and the way to behave according to what others think or say.

Then we were thrust into the adult world and found that things really do change and we had to adapt or lose a job, friends, shelter and habits in order to fit in or be left out. We found our inner self, our personality, telling us we would be better off being a better person, a better friend, a better lover.

When we fought back with ourselves about whether we should

even be good, let alone better, our life-force, our soul, reminded us how we had formed habits and preached that if we didn't do good, we'd lose it (we didn't need a Jiminy Cricket to tell us that!).

As we found ourselves being praised for our accomplishments as a person, we freely acknowledged our ability to be ourselves and do what we want to do, even denying that there is an "ever" because we know that nothing lasts forever on this earth, using that as an excuse to pardon our forays into doing evil.

So if our inclinations toward evil resulted in taking advantage or doing harm to others, we congratulated ourselves on being smart enough to ignore guilt because our own good deserved everything we could get and enjoy in the present.

Our life-force, our soul, struck back, telling us that if we don't believe and trust in others, we won't find faith and trust in ourselves.

At first, our rational self pointed out that our strength was in ourselves. We firmly believed and trusted our ability to do things for just us. That nagging moment of hesitation dredged our imagination and emotions to bring up times and events where failure and denial to ourselves weakened and almost destroyed our own trust and assurance.

Our life-force, our soul, in one final attempt, reminded us the choice is ours: is this other person worth as much to us as we are to ourselves?

Now the forever deniers can come back and say: if there is a heaven, it's going to be boring because, without body and mind, there won't be free will and there won't be choices because everything will be good and there will be no evil. In other words, no body, no pleasure, no temptation.

Adam and Eve had free will and they got kicked out of paradise for doing the wrong thing. Have they and we found joy in evil? If we are to be happy forever, then we can be happy that there is no evil in heaven. Evil is down in hell where bad people and bad angels are. They can keep abusing each other forever while the good people enjoy being with and helping each other. We have a choice of venues.

Chapter Eight

If heaven is such a great place, why not kill ourselves and get there sooner? After all, some people die sooner than others. Why not leave this earth and enjoy heaven sooner? Some people like to have wars and kill thousands and millions because winning is everything, just like a game.

Some people like to think that's why some people commit suicide.

But it seems that people commit suicide because they are depressed with life. Many believe that things won't get better because they have lost faith and trust in others, thereby losing faith and trust in themselves. They force themselves away from that moment of hesitation because they believe that all is lost and there is no way out except self destruction of body and mind, not realizing the soul is giving them an out.

Some people criticize psychiatrists, blaming them for not countering suicides. The critics probably are not aware of the mind-changing medications that have become available for psychiatrists to prescribe to alleviate aberrant behavior and some abnormalities that have allowed caregivers an easier regimen at brief interludes and many times for longer duration instead of constantly watching and being prepared at all times to deal with sometimes violent behavior or worrisome confusion.

Laboratory studies have mapped areas of the brain so we get a clearer picture of activity governing sections which have helped in the development of medications and a better understanding of where activity triggers are. But just the word "Alzheimer's" arouses fear in aging seniors and middle-aged males and females.

Heaven isn't thirsting for our arrival there. We are tested in this existence to try and learn how to care for and share with other persons.

We have all kinds of wit to remind us we can get there, like "Where there's a will, there's a way" and "Things can get better if you make them so".

But most impressive is the fact that we are living longer. We can see our children, grandchildren and even great-grandchildren grow into adulthood.

Living longer gives us the opportunity to work to make things better instead of complaining, like the majority, that we are helpless to do things because we haven't got the time.

Whom we call seniors have seen companies ridding themselves of many employees and finding that customer service is almost non-existent and no training is provided for the employees that are newly-hired so that there seems to be less organization and less dedication to the company, resulting in employee turnover. Any downturns in the stock market worry those seniors who receive regular stock dividends because how long can the good times last and the dividends remain high or last? Their memories remind them of too many financial recessions since the last great war.

The polling numbers are showing that people aged 55 and over turn out the most for off-presidential year elections to vote. More must be done to reach the politicians in charge of government. Petitions and e-mails are turning out to be the most effective means of communication in our fractured society and are forcing more seniors to get familiar with electronic tablets, android cell phones and computers.

So far what has changed some laws and attitudes have been opinion polls with the results broadcast on TV and in the newspapers. There are topics brought up for consideration through opinion polls and controversies abound.

Controversy breeds change. Because of low wages or lack of employment chances or regional changes in work interests, many young adults may have moved in with their parents but now they want to move out and away since family ties are looser and the economy is more diversified depending on employment preferences and where work is located.

Since military service may have afforded opportunities to live in different locales, many young deadlocked adults now want to be near oceans or lakes or near mountains or gentle hills.

Not just older adults want to live in warmer climates to avoid winter yet some young adults want to live in northern climates where there is a change of seasons. Migration patterns are diverse even with the high cost of homes and apartments.

American culture still has diversities but the mix has homogenized so that people can find a neighborhood to fit into.

A senior person no longer concerned with work finds a choice, either to remain active or to relegate oneself to being passive. For those with sufficient savings and income, travel seems to appeal to many. After a few journeys, depending on expenses and depletion of funds, there can be a diminishing of desire to travel or some can still afford the wanderlust.

For those with limited income or a physical hindrance, a more sedentary lifestyle may happen although social relationships can afford an active social life.

As people age, the less they want to be classified, especially naming any class they might be assigned to by the media. The opinion polls still get away with numbering results according to age but still have to allow for broad categories (e.g. 45-55, 65 +, 70 and beyond).

There seems to be a minimizing of the 55-65 category because the period of 1950 to 1960 encompassed the Korean War, an uneasy truce and a long recession, even though the freeways were being built. The baby boom didn't start until the late 1950's so the 60 to 65 year old are the ones neglected by Congress by having to wait for full Social Security retirement until age 66 and Medicare at age 65.

By taking Social Security at age 62, they lose a considerable percentage of retirement income with the promise of making it up to them in their age 70's. They had to endure crowded classrooms and a shortage of teachers because the nation concentrated on cars and homes and roads instead of schools and education.

To even try to mention differences between senior citizen males and females requires a pardon for the indulgence to discuss broad generalities. Remember that we all are individuals and we all have free will so we all are free to act as we want.

Males tend to be loners with narrow categories of topics for discussion whereas females tend to have a bevy of friends and a willingness to discuss many topics and like to be around other persons and be more involved with their families and grandchildren.

Hopefully, in the near future, both male and female seniors will have to consider giving up their cars for transportation because of rising costs of maintenance and vehicle replacement so that they use bicycles and motor scooters which may have them exercising more. If only government would get back to working in behalf of its citizens, especially senior citizens, so that transportation problems would be solved at least within the next decade, if not sooner.

Modern electronics, like the cell phone, computer and tablet have improved communication for seniors as well as for persons of all ages. Unfortunately, the electronics are making face-to-face contact (except by video) almost nonexistent. For all the cameras on cell phones, even picture-taking seems to be recording for storing in picture albums or on some flash drive.

The use of e-mails on those electronic devices have made communications faster and easier but the lack of handwriting in cursive makes one wonder if the cult of personality is being lost by not showing one's ability to express oneself by one's own hand with flourish and careful consideration of word usage instead of quick abbreviated notes with cryptic word parts and letters. There are too many grandchildren of seniors today that can't read the documents that are responsible for founding this country.

What is of most concern for seniors today is their health. The majority of seniors want to live longer and to be healthy. Health is defined as the condition of being sound in body, mind and spirit.

For the body, that means free from disease and pain. Modern medicine has made dramatic improvements in the treatment of cancer, polio, whooping cough, diphtheria, typhoid and infant mortality. Transplanting organs has extended many people's lives. Medications have helped to control pain. Anesthesia has made difficult operations possible so that a patient doesn't have to bite on a stick to eliminate screams of pain. Needles and catheters have allowed for delivering necessary medications or for removing waste from the body or providing sustenance for comatose patients. The length of hospital stays has been reduced. Medications are extending the lives of people with heart problems or various other ills.

For the mind, that means the ability to reason, to make a judgment and to remember. For the brain, that means avoiding concussions and the desire to learn in order to improve thinking, doing and communicating while controlling the various functions of the body to keep the organs active. We have billions of brain cells tucked into that little head of ours to keep life going in our body. When many die off daily, they are replaced to keep us going.

For the spirit, that is the vital principle that gives life to our physical organs. It is the essence of our being. It is the spiritual embedded cause of our existence on this earth. It is our soul, our life-force, our actual cause for being here. It isn't that slap on the back that the nurse gives us to get the lungs working with that first breath of oxygen. We generally came out tussling and crying out to announce that we were here. We were born to be here in order to fulfill our mission to die here. When we leave, our body stays here but our spirit doesn't because it's the cause of our being here first.

People with a cause that had a leader remark that the person's spirit reminds them of their leader and energizes their cause. History reminds us of the leaders of the cause for a free America. The cause is evidence of the spirit of their actions that resulted in the founding of the United States. Why do people want to deny the spirit of the cause? Because they are free to do it. They have free will, not just because government lets them but because their Creator gave them it in their spirit. To deny people the freedom to come here to be free is being free to deny them but not caring for the persons who want to come here. Confusing, but we have a mind that can reason even in confusion.

What is confusing to many seniors is the lack of caring and sharing for not only seniors but for all age groups today. With all the improvements in health for body, mind and spirit, there is a lack of concern on the part of some people that all should share in these blessings.

According to the polls, over half of the country is opposed to a law that says to take care of your health. The media does have an undue amount of influence on people's thinking even to creating slander. Once honor and truth are called into question on trumped up charges, there is no redemption, as in the Dreyfus affair in France following assignation about a person's religion influencing their actions, and today when a statesman is threatened with treason where there was none.

Instead of a war on mental illness in order to come up with extensive proper treatment, the government prefers to spend billions of dollars on instruments of war with methods that are out of date with the times when small groups of terrorists are the threat rather than vast armies of soldiers.

Polls are indicating a greater and greater decline in belief in and practice of religion. It's said that religion is old-fashioned and not necessary to practice it. We build monuments to cover the places where thousands have died and we forget the millions of people who died in the two great wars of the 20th century.

There are fewer and fewer survivors of atomic warfare and few are concerned about the radiation from disasters where nature was contaminated.

Radiation can be a death-force. You can't see it but it can kill you. Death-force doesn't allow for free will. If you are in its path, too bad. There's no escape. The death-force is a man-made creation. You don't have to believe about it. But its effects are hideous and horrendous.

Chapter Nine

A psychiatrist could easily say "You've got to be nuts to be good" after dealing with the anxieties, scruples, emotions, compulsions and virtues acting on an individual possessing free will.

If you were conscious, why did you do it? If you were unconscious, why did it happen?

All these considerations are so mind-bending that psychiatrists tend to have a higher suicide rate than other physicians.

What of those persons advanced in age who realize that death can happen at any time and think of those times in life that wrongs were done?

Since life is given to us, it is reasonable to suspect that our conscious self is aware of those wrongs. Dementia and Alzheimer's disease will allow our unconscious selves to operate without reason or thinking ability. The fear of losing memory and reason terrifies our conscious self so there must be something compelling our inner self to want to hold onto its judgment-making ability.

The body hopes that medication will prolong life. The mind tells it that death is inevitable. The body and mind will both fight for life. Life support machines can continue life but infection somehow happens and the organs succumb.

Freezing the body and its organs seems to be turning out to be like frozen dinners: once thawed they're not like fresh because they don't hold up well the longer they're frozen.

As we get close to death, we seek peace: peaceful living and a peaceful death. The threat of pain and disease interrupt peace. Medication can control pain and ease the transition to death.

It's difficult to try and convince many people that things like life insurance, setting up trusts, grants and wills should be taken care of far in advance of the threat of death and senior aging. These things take into account wealth and property distribution so relatives, hopefully, won't argue about these things before or after a person's death.

There is even something that is called an advance health care directive which has to do with whether or not a person wishes to donate his/her organs after death so other ill persons can have replacements for failing organs. The directive also instructs whether the deceased's body is to be used for medical study or is to be cremated or buried.

Most importantly, the person having the directive instructs whether he/she should be resuscitated or allowed to die since machines can continue life for a long time but it isn't a thinking and acting living.

Regardless of how rich and powerful a person was in life, death makes us all equal in ending our existence on this earth. Great monuments have been built to honor certain people but time erodes the memories of them so that only books with remnants of their words and events may still remain.

Empires can be divided up . Governments and religions can be changed. Our universe will one day cease to be. Our physical beings will become ash or dirt.

Deep inside us a voice speaks silently in our ear. You have to answer for your life to the Eternal Judge. Whether ready or not, you will have to answer for it.

Conscience and free will were given to you. What have you given in return?

There is no end now.

Table of Contents

47

43